50 BBQ Packed Recipes for Home

By: Kelly Johnson

Table of Contents

- BBQ Pulled Pork Sandwiches
- Smoked Brisket
- Grilled Baby Back Ribs
- BBQ Chicken Wings
- Grilled Portobello Mushrooms
- Barbecue Meatballs
- BBQ Beef Short Ribs
- Grilled Shrimp Skewers
- BBQ Bacon-Wrapped Jalapeño Poppers
- Cedar-Plank Salmon
- BBQ Pork Belly Burnt Ends
- Grilled Veggie Kabobs
- Texas-Style Smoked Sausage
- BBQ Lamb Chops
- Spicy BBQ Chicken Drumsticks
- Carolina Pulled Pork
- Grilled Corn on the Cob with Chili Butter
- BBQ Chicken Pizza
- Beer Can Chicken
- Grilled Pineapple Slices
- Barbecue Tofu Skewers
- BBQ Glazed Meatloaf
- Smoked Turkey Legs
- BBQ Baked Beans
- Grilled Steak Fajitas
- Sticky BBQ Ribs
- Smoked Salmon Tacos
- BBQ Beef Burgers
- BBQ Chicken Nachos
- Grilled Lobster Tails
- Korean BBQ Short Ribs (Galbi)
- Barbecue Pork Chops
- Grilled Zucchini Boats
- BBQ Jackfruit Sandwiches
- Smoked Brisket Chili

- Barbecue Glazed Shrimp Tacos
- Grilled Flatbread with BBQ Sauce
- BBQ Chicken Kebabs
- Smoked Pulled Pork Quesadillas
- Grilled Peaches with Honey Glaze
- BBQ Pork Riblets
- Charcoal-Grilled Steaks with Garlic Butter
- BBQ Buffalo Cauliflower Bites
- Smoked Mac and Cheese
- BBQ Brisket Sandwiches with Slaw
- Grilled Chicken Caesar Salad
- Barbecue Glazed Meatball Subs
- BBQ Veggie Pizza
- Grilled Oysters with Garlic Butter
- BBQ Chicken and Cornbread Casserole

BBQ Pulled Pork Sandwiches

Ingredients

- 4 lbs pork shoulder (Boston butt)
- 1 tablespoon paprika
- 1 teaspoon garlic powder
- 1 teaspoon onion powder
- 1 teaspoon salt
- ½ teaspoon pepper
- 1 cup BBQ sauce
- ½ cup apple cider vinegar
- 1 onion, sliced
- 8 sandwich buns
- Coleslaw (optional)

Instructions

1. **Season Pork:**
   - Rub the pork shoulder with paprika, garlic powder, onion powder, salt, and pepper.
2. **Cook:**
   - Place the pork, onion, and vinegar in a slow cooker. Cook on low for 8-10 hours or until tender.
3. **Shred and Sauce:**
   - Shred the pork with two forks and stir in BBQ sauce.
4. **Assemble Sandwiches:**
   - Serve the pulled pork on buns, topped with coleslaw if desired.

Smoked Brisket

Ingredients

- 5-6 lbs beef brisket
- 2 tablespoons kosher salt
- 1 tablespoon black pepper
- 2 tablespoons paprika
- 2 teaspoons garlic powder
- Wood chips for smoking (hickory or oak)

Instructions

1. **Season Brisket:**
    - Rub the brisket with salt, pepper, paprika, and garlic powder.
2. **Smoke:**
    - Preheat the smoker to 225°F (107°C). Smoke brisket for 10-12 hours or until internal temperature reaches 195-205°F (90-96°C).
3. **Rest and Serve:**
    - Wrap brisket in foil and let rest for 30 minutes. Slice against the grain to serve.

Grilled Baby Back Ribs

Ingredients

- 2 racks baby back ribs
- ¼ cup brown sugar
- 2 tablespoons paprika
- 1 teaspoon black pepper
- 1 teaspoon garlic powder
- ½ teaspoon cayenne pepper
- BBQ sauce

Instructions

1. **Prepare Ribs:**
    - Remove the membrane from the back of the ribs. Rub with the seasoning mix.
2. **Grill:**
    - Wrap ribs in foil and grill over indirect heat at 300°F (150°C) for 2-3 hours.
3. **Finish with Sauce:**
    - Unwrap, brush with BBQ sauce, and grill for 15 minutes over direct heat.

BBQ Chicken Wings

Ingredients

- 2 lbs chicken wings
- 1 tablespoon olive oil
- 1 teaspoon salt
- 1 teaspoon black pepper
- ½ teaspoon garlic powder
- 1 cup BBQ sauce

Instructions

1. **Season Wings:**
    - Toss wings in olive oil, salt, pepper, and garlic powder.
2. **Grill:**
    - Grill over medium heat for 20-25 minutes, turning occasionally.
3. **Add Sauce:**
    - Brush with BBQ sauce and grill for another 5 minutes.

Grilled Portobello Mushrooms

Ingredients

- 4 large Portobello mushrooms
- ¼ cup olive oil
- 2 tablespoons balsamic vinegar
- 2 cloves garlic, minced
- Salt and pepper to taste

Instructions

1. **Marinate Mushrooms:**
    - Mix olive oil, vinegar, garlic, salt, and pepper. Marinate mushrooms for 30 minutes.
2. **Grill:**
    - Grill mushrooms for 4-5 minutes on each side over medium heat.

Barbecue Meatballs

Ingredients

- 1 lb ground beef
- ½ cup breadcrumbs
- 1 egg
- 2 cloves garlic, minced
- Salt and pepper to taste
- 1 cup BBQ sauce

Instructions

1. **Make Meatballs:**
    - Mix beef, breadcrumbs, egg, garlic, salt, and pepper. Form into 1-inch meatballs.
2. **Cook:**
    - Bake at 375°F (190°C) for 20 minutes. Toss with BBQ sauce.

BBQ Beef Short Ribs

Ingredients

- 3 lbs beef short ribs
- Salt and pepper
- 1 onion, sliced
- 2 cups BBQ sauce

Instructions

1. **Season and Sear:**
   - Season ribs with salt and pepper. Sear in a hot pan.
2. **Slow Cook:**
   - Place ribs and onions in a slow cooker. Pour in BBQ sauce and cook on low for 8 hours.
3. **Serve:**
   - Serve with extra sauce on the side.

Grilled Shrimp Skewers

Ingredients

- 1 lb large shrimp, peeled and deveined
- ¼ cup olive oil
- 2 tablespoons lemon juice
- 2 cloves garlic, minced
- Salt and pepper to taste

Instructions

1. **Marinate Shrimp:**
    - Mix olive oil, lemon juice, garlic, salt, and pepper. Marinate shrimp for 15 minutes.
2. **Skewer and Grill:**
    - Thread shrimp onto skewers and grill for 2-3 minutes per side over medium-high heat.

BBQ Bacon-Wrapped Jalapeño Poppers

Ingredients

- 12 jalapeños, halved and seeded
- 8 oz cream cheese, softened
- 1 cup shredded cheddar cheese
- 12 slices of bacon, halved
- BBQ sauce for brushing

Instructions

1. **Fill Jalapeños:**
    - Mix cream cheese and cheddar. Fill each jalapeño half with the mixture.
2. **Wrap and Grill:**
    - Wrap each popper with half a slice of bacon. Grill over medium heat for 8-10 minutes, turning often.
3. **Add Sauce:**
    - Brush with BBQ sauce during the last 2 minutes of grilling.

Cedar-Plank Salmon

Ingredients

- 2 lbs salmon fillet
- ¼ cup olive oil
- 2 tablespoons lemon juice
- 2 garlic cloves, minced
- 1 teaspoon salt
- Cedar plank (soaked in water for 1 hour)

Instructions

1. **Prepare Salmon:**
    - Combine olive oil, lemon juice, garlic, and salt. Marinate salmon for 30 minutes.
2. **Grill:**
    - Place salmon on the soaked cedar plank and grill over indirect heat for 20-25 minutes until flaky.

BBQ Pork Belly Burnt Ends

Ingredients

- 3 lbs pork belly, cubed
- 2 tablespoons BBQ rub
- ½ cup BBQ sauce
- ¼ cup honey

Instructions

1. **Season and Smoke:**
   - Rub pork belly with BBQ rub and smoke at 250°F (120°C) for 2-3 hours.
2. **Sauce:**
   - Toss with BBQ sauce and honey. Return to the smoker for 30 minutes until caramelized.

Grilled Veggie Kabobs

Ingredients

- 2 zucchinis, sliced
- 2 bell peppers, cubed
- 1 red onion, chopped
- ¼ cup olive oil
- 2 tablespoons balsamic vinegar
- Salt and pepper to taste

Instructions

1. **Prepare Veggies:**
    - Toss veggies with olive oil, vinegar, salt, and pepper.
2. **Grill:**
    - Thread onto skewers and grill over medium heat for 10-12 minutes, turning occasionally.

Texas-Style Smoked Sausage

Ingredients

- 2 lbs smoked sausage links
- ½ cup BBQ sauce
- 1 tablespoon mustard

Instructions

1. **Grill Sausages:**
   - Grill sausages over medium heat for 6-8 minutes, turning frequently.
2. **Glaze:**
   - Brush with a mixture of BBQ sauce and mustard during the last 2 minutes.

BBQ Lamb Chops

Ingredients

- 8 lamb chops
- ¼ cup olive oil
- 2 tablespoons rosemary, chopped
- 2 garlic cloves, minced
- Salt and pepper to taste

Instructions

1. **Marinate Chops:**
    - Mix olive oil, rosemary, garlic, salt, and pepper. Marinate lamb chops for 1 hour.
2. **Grill:**
    - Grill for 3-4 minutes per side over medium-high heat.

Spicy BBQ Chicken Drumsticks

Ingredients

- 12 chicken drumsticks
- 1 tablespoon olive oil
- 1 teaspoon cayenne pepper
- 1 teaspoon smoked paprika
- 1 cup BBQ sauce

Instructions

1. **Season Chicken:**
    - Toss drumsticks with olive oil, cayenne, and paprika.
2. **Grill:**
    - Grill for 20-25 minutes over medium heat, turning often.
3. **Add Sauce:**
    - Brush with BBQ sauce during the last 5 minutes.

Carolina Pulled Pork

Ingredients

- 4 lbs pork shoulder
- 1 tablespoon mustard
- 2 tablespoons brown sugar
- 1 tablespoon paprika
- 1 teaspoon cayenne
- 1 cup apple cider vinegar
- 1 cup Carolina BBQ sauce

Instructions

1. **Season Pork:**
    - Rub pork with mustard, brown sugar, paprika, and cayenne.
2. **Smoke:**
    - Smoke at 225°F (107°C) for 8-10 hours until tender.
3. **Shred and Sauce:**
    - Shred the pork and toss with apple cider vinegar and Carolina BBQ sauce.

Grilled Corn on the Cob with Chili Butter

Ingredients

- 4 ears of corn, husked
- ½ cup unsalted butter, softened
- 1 teaspoon chili powder
- ½ teaspoon smoked paprika
- Salt to taste
- Lime wedges for serving

Instructions

1. **Prepare Butter:**
    - In a bowl, mix softened butter with chili powder, smoked paprika, and salt.
2. **Grill Corn:**
    - Preheat the grill to medium-high. Grill corn for 10-15 minutes, turning occasionally.
3. **Serve:**
    - Spread chili butter on grilled corn and serve with lime wedges.

BBQ Chicken Pizza

Ingredients

- 1 pre-made pizza crust
- 1 cup cooked chicken, shredded
- ½ cup BBQ sauce
- 1 cup mozzarella cheese, shredded
- ½ red onion, thinly sliced
- Fresh cilantro for garnish

Instructions

1. **Preheat Oven:**
    - Preheat oven according to pizza crust instructions.
2. **Assemble Pizza:**
    - Mix shredded chicken with BBQ sauce. Spread on the crust, top with mozzarella and red onion.
3. **Bake:**
    - Bake for 12-15 minutes or until the cheese is bubbly. Garnish with cilantro before serving.

Beer Can Chicken

Ingredients

- 1 whole chicken (about 4-5 lbs)
- 1 can of beer (or soda)
- 2 tablespoons olive oil
- 1 tablespoon garlic powder
- 1 tablespoon paprika
- Salt and pepper to taste

Instructions

1. **Prepare Chicken:**
    - Rub chicken with olive oil, garlic powder, paprika, salt, and pepper.
2. **Insert Beer Can:**
    - Open the can of beer and place it inside the chicken cavity.
3. **Grill:**
    - Place the chicken upright on the grill and cook for 1.5-2 hours until the internal temperature reaches 165°F (75°C).

Grilled Pineapple Slices

Ingredients

- 1 fresh pineapple, peeled and sliced into rings
- 2 tablespoons brown sugar
- 1 teaspoon cinnamon

Instructions

1. **Prepare Pineapple:**
    - Sprinkle brown sugar and cinnamon over pineapple slices.
2. **Grill:**
    - Preheat grill to medium heat. Grill pineapple for 3-4 minutes per side until caramelized.

Barbecue Tofu Skewers

Ingredients

- 1 block firm tofu, drained and pressed
- ½ cup BBQ sauce
- 1 bell pepper, cubed
- 1 red onion, cubed
- Skewers

Instructions

1. **Marinate Tofu:**
    - Cut tofu into cubes and marinate in BBQ sauce for at least 30 minutes.
2. **Assemble Skewers:**
    - Thread tofu, bell pepper, and onion onto skewers.
3. **Grill:**
    - Grill over medium heat for 10-15 minutes, brushing with extra BBQ sauce.

BBQ Glazed Meatloaf

Ingredients

- 1 lb ground beef
- 1 cup breadcrumbs
- 1 egg
- ½ cup onion, finely chopped
- ½ cup BBQ sauce (plus extra for glazing)
- Salt and pepper to taste

Instructions

1. **Preheat Oven:**
   - Preheat oven to 350°F (175°C).
2. **Mix Ingredients:**
   - In a bowl, combine ground beef, breadcrumbs, egg, onion, BBQ sauce, salt, and pepper.
3. **Shape and Bake:**
   - Shape mixture into a loaf and place in a baking dish. Brush with BBQ sauce and bake for 1 hour.

Smoked Turkey Legs

Ingredients

- 4 turkey legs
- 2 tablespoons olive oil
- 2 tablespoons smoked paprika
- 1 tablespoon garlic powder
- Salt and pepper to taste

Instructions

1. **Prepare Turkey Legs:**
    - Rub turkey legs with olive oil, smoked paprika, garlic powder, salt, and pepper.
2. **Smoke:**
    - Smoke at 225°F (107°C) for 2-3 hours until the internal temperature reaches 165°F (75°C).

BBQ Baked Beans

Ingredients

- 2 cans (15 oz each) baked beans
- ½ cup BBQ sauce
- ¼ cup brown sugar
- 1 small onion, diced
- 1 tablespoon mustard

Instructions

1. **Combine Ingredients:**
     - In a pot, combine baked beans, BBQ sauce, brown sugar, onion, and mustard.
2. **Bake:**
     - Transfer to a baking dish and bake at 350°F (175°C) for 30-40 minutes until heated through and slightly thickened.

Grilled Steak Fajitas

Ingredients

- 1 lb flank steak
- 2 tablespoons olive oil
- 1 tablespoon lime juice
- 1 teaspoon cumin
- 1 teaspoon chili powder
- 1 bell pepper, sliced
- 1 onion, sliced
- Flour tortillas
- Salsa and sour cream for serving

Instructions

1. **Marinate Steak:**
     - Combine olive oil, lime juice, cumin, chili powder, and steak in a zip-top bag. Marinate for at least 30 minutes.
2. **Grill Steak:**
     - Preheat grill to medium-high. Grill steak for 5-7 minutes per side for medium-rare. Let it rest before slicing.
3. **Sauté Vegetables:**
     - In a skillet, sauté bell pepper and onion until softened.
4. **Serve:**
     - Slice steak and serve in tortillas with sautéed vegetables, salsa, and sour cream.

Sticky BBQ Ribs

Ingredients

- 2 racks baby back ribs
- 1 cup BBQ sauce
- 1 tablespoon brown sugar
- 1 tablespoon apple cider vinegar
- 1 teaspoon garlic powder
- Salt and pepper to taste

Instructions

1. **Prepare Ribs:**
   - Preheat oven to 300°F (150°C). Season ribs with salt and pepper.
2. **Cook Ribs:**
   - Place ribs on a baking sheet and cover tightly with foil. Bake for 2.5-3 hours until tender.
3. **Glaze and Grill:**
   - Mix BBQ sauce, brown sugar, and apple cider vinegar. Brush sauce on ribs and grill for 10-15 minutes until sticky.

Smoked Salmon Tacos

Ingredients

- 8 small corn tortillas
- 8 oz smoked salmon
- 1 avocado, sliced
- ½ cup cream cheese
- 1 tablespoon capers
- Fresh dill for garnish

Instructions

1. **Warm Tortillas:**
    - Warm tortillas on a grill or stovetop.
2. **Assemble Tacos:**
    - Spread cream cheese on each tortilla, top with smoked salmon, avocado slices, and capers.
3. **Serve:**
    - Garnish with fresh dill and serve.

BBQ Beef Burgers

Ingredients

- 1 lb ground beef
- ¼ cup BBQ sauce
- 1 teaspoon garlic powder
- 1 teaspoon onion powder
- Salt and pepper to taste
- Burger buns
- Toppings: lettuce, tomato, cheese

Instructions

1. **Mix Ingredients:**
    - In a bowl, combine ground beef, BBQ sauce, garlic powder, onion powder, salt, and pepper.
2. **Form Patties:**
    - Shape mixture into patties.
3. **Grill Patties:**
    - Preheat grill to medium-high and grill patties for 5-7 minutes per side, until cooked to your liking. Serve on buns with toppings.

BBQ Chicken Nachos

Ingredients

- 2 cups tortilla chips
- 1 cup shredded cooked chicken
- ½ cup BBQ sauce
- 1 cup shredded cheese (cheddar or Monterey Jack)
- ½ cup jalapeños (optional)
- Sour cream and green onions for serving

Instructions

1. **Preheat Oven:**
   - Preheat oven to 350°F (175°C).
2. **Prepare Nachos:**
   - On a baking sheet, layer tortilla chips, shredded chicken mixed with BBQ sauce, and cheese.
3. **Bake:**
   - Bake for 10-15 minutes until cheese is melted. Top with jalapeños, sour cream, and green onions.

Grilled Lobster Tails

Ingredients

- 4 lobster tails
- 4 tablespoons butter, melted
- 2 tablespoons lemon juice
- 1 teaspoon garlic, minced
- Salt and pepper to taste

Instructions

1. **Prepare Lobster:**
   - Preheat grill to medium heat. Cut lobster tails in half lengthwise.
2. **Make Butter Sauce:**
   - Mix melted butter, lemon juice, garlic, salt, and pepper.
3. **Grill Lobster:**
   - Brush lobster with butter mixture and grill for 5-7 minutes until the meat is opaque.

Korean BBQ Short Ribs (Galbi)

Ingredients

- 2 lbs beef short ribs
- ½ cup soy sauce
- ¼ cup brown sugar
- 2 tablespoons sesame oil
- 3 cloves garlic, minced
- 1 tablespoon ginger, minced
- 1 tablespoon rice vinegar

Instructions

1. **Marinate Ribs:**
    - In a bowl, mix soy sauce, brown sugar, sesame oil, garlic, ginger, and rice vinegar. Marinate ribs for at least 2 hours, preferably overnight.
2. **Grill Ribs:**
    - Preheat grill to medium-high. Grill short ribs for 3-5 minutes per side until cooked through.

Barbecue Pork Chops

Ingredients

- 4 pork chops
- 1 cup BBQ sauce
- 1 tablespoon olive oil
- Salt and pepper to taste

Instructions

1. **Season Pork Chops:**
    - Rub pork chops with olive oil, salt, and pepper.
2. **Grill Chops:**
    - Preheat grill to medium heat. Grill pork chops for 6-7 minutes per side.
3. **Glaze with BBQ Sauce:**
    - During the last few minutes of cooking, brush with BBQ sauce and grill until caramelized.

Grilled Zucchini Boats

Ingredients

- 4 medium zucchinis
- 1 cup cooked quinoa
- 1 cup cherry tomatoes, halved
- 1 cup shredded mozzarella cheese
- 1 teaspoon Italian seasoning
- Salt and pepper to taste
- Olive oil for drizzling

Instructions

1. **Prepare Zucchini:**
    - Preheat grill to medium heat. Cut zucchinis in half lengthwise and scoop out the seeds to create boats.
2. **Mix Filling:**
    - In a bowl, combine cooked quinoa, cherry tomatoes, mozzarella, Italian seasoning, salt, and pepper.
3. **Fill Zucchini:**
    - Spoon filling into the zucchini halves and drizzle with olive oil.
4. **Grill:**
    - Grill for 10-15 minutes until zucchini is tender and cheese is melted.

BBQ Jackfruit Sandwiches

Ingredients

- 2 cans young green jackfruit in brine, drained and rinsed
- 1 cup BBQ sauce
- 1 tablespoon olive oil
- 1 onion, chopped
- Burger buns
- Coleslaw for topping

Instructions

1. **Prepare Jackfruit:**
    - Heat olive oil in a skillet over medium heat. Add chopped onion and sauté until translucent.
2. **Cook Jackfruit:**
    - Add jackfruit to the skillet, breaking it apart with a fork. Stir in BBQ sauce and cook for 15-20 minutes, until heated through and well combined.
3. **Serve:**
    - Serve jackfruit mixture on burger buns topped with coleslaw.

Smoked Brisket Chili

Ingredients

- 2 cups smoked brisket, chopped
- 1 can (28 oz) diced tomatoes
- 1 can (15 oz) kidney beans, drained and rinsed
- 1 can (15 oz) black beans, drained and rinsed
- 1 onion, chopped
- 2 cloves garlic, minced
- 1 tablespoon chili powder
- 1 teaspoon cumin
- Salt and pepper to taste

Instructions

1. **Sauté Vegetables:**
    - In a large pot, sauté chopped onion and garlic until soft.
2. **Combine Ingredients:**
    - Add smoked brisket, diced tomatoes, beans, chili powder, cumin, salt, and pepper.
3. **Simmer:**
    - Bring to a boil, then reduce heat and simmer for 30 minutes. Adjust seasoning as needed.

Barbecue Glazed Shrimp Tacos

Ingredients

- 1 lb shrimp, peeled and deveined
- ½ cup BBQ sauce
- 8 small corn tortillas
- 1 avocado, sliced
- ½ cup shredded cabbage
- Lime wedges for serving

Instructions

1. **Marinate Shrimp:**
    - Toss shrimp in BBQ sauce and let marinate for 15 minutes.
2. **Grill Shrimp:**
    - Preheat grill to medium-high. Grill shrimp for 2-3 minutes per side until cooked through.
3. **Assemble Tacos:**
    - Serve shrimp in tortillas topped with avocado and cabbage. Squeeze lime over tacos before serving.

Grilled Flatbread with BBQ Sauce

Ingredients

- 1 store-bought flatbread or naan
- ½ cup BBQ sauce
- 1 cup shredded cheese (cheddar or mozzarella)
- 1 cup cooked chicken or pulled pork (optional)
- Sliced red onion and cilantro for topping

Instructions

1. **Preheat Grill:**
   - Preheat grill to medium heat.
2. **Assemble Flatbread:**
   - Spread BBQ sauce over the flatbread, sprinkle cheese, and add cooked chicken or pulled pork if using.
3. **Grill Flatbread:**
   - Grill for 5-7 minutes until cheese is melted and bubbly. Top with sliced red onion and cilantro before serving.

BBQ Chicken Kebabs

Ingredients

- 1 lb chicken breast, cubed
- 1 bell pepper, cut into chunks
- 1 red onion, cut into chunks
- ½ cup BBQ sauce
- Skewers (wooden or metal)
- Salt and pepper to taste

Instructions

1. **Prepare Kebabs:**
   - In a bowl, toss chicken, bell pepper, and onion with BBQ sauce, salt, and pepper.
2. **Assemble Skewers:**
   - Thread chicken and vegetables onto skewers.
3. **Grill Kebabs:**
   - Preheat grill to medium-high and grill kebabs for 10-12 minutes, turning occasionally until chicken is cooked through.

Smoked Pulled Pork Quesadillas

Ingredients

- 2 cups smoked pulled pork
- 1 cup shredded cheese (cheddar or Monterey Jack)
- 4 large flour tortillas
- 1 cup BBQ sauce
- Sour cream and salsa for serving

Instructions

1. **Prepare Quesadillas:**
    - Heat a skillet over medium heat. On half of each tortilla, layer pulled pork, cheese, and a drizzle of BBQ sauce. Fold tortillas in half.
2. **Cook Quesadillas:**
    - Cook each quesadilla for 3-4 minutes per side until golden brown and cheese is melted.
3. **Serve:**
    - Cut into wedges and serve with sour cream and salsa.

Grilled Peaches with Honey Glaze

Ingredients

- 4 ripe peaches, halved and pitted
- 2 tablespoons honey
- 1 tablespoon olive oil
- Cinnamon for sprinkling (optional)

Instructions

1. **Prepare Peaches:**
   - Preheat grill to medium heat. In a small bowl, mix honey and olive oil.
2. **Glaze Peaches:**
   - Brush cut sides of peaches with honey mixture.
3. **Grill Peaches:**
   - Place peaches cut-side down on the grill and grill for 4-5 minutes until caramelized. Sprinkle with cinnamon before serving.

BBQ Pork Riblets

Ingredients

- 2 lbs pork riblets
- 1 cup BBQ sauce
- 2 tablespoons brown sugar
- 1 tablespoon paprika
- 1 teaspoon garlic powder
- 1 teaspoon onion powder
- Salt and pepper to taste

Instructions

1. **Preheat Oven:**
   - Preheat oven to 300°F (150°C).
2. **Season Riblets:**
   - In a bowl, mix brown sugar, paprika, garlic powder, onion powder, salt, and pepper. Rub this mixture all over the riblets.
3. **Bake:**
   - Place riblets on a baking sheet lined with foil and cover tightly with another sheet of foil. Bake for 2-2.5 hours until tender.
4. **Grill:**
   - Preheat grill to medium heat. Brush riblets with BBQ sauce and grill for 5-7 minutes, basting with more sauce, until caramelized.

Charcoal-Grilled Steaks with Garlic Butter

Ingredients

- 2 ribeye or sirloin steaks
- 4 tablespoons unsalted butter, softened
- 4 cloves garlic, minced
- Salt and pepper to taste
- Fresh herbs (rosemary or thyme) for garnish

Instructions

1. **Prepare Garlic Butter:**
    - In a bowl, combine softened butter, minced garlic, salt, and pepper. Mix well and set aside.
2. **Season Steaks:**
    - Season steaks generously with salt and pepper.
3. **Grill Steaks:**
    - Preheat charcoal grill to high heat. Grill steaks for 4-5 minutes per side for medium-rare, or until desired doneness.
4. **Serve:**
    - Top steaks with garlic butter and garnish with fresh herbs before serving.

BBQ Buffalo Cauliflower Bites

Ingredients

- 1 head cauliflower, cut into florets
- ½ cup buffalo sauce
- ½ cup flour
- 1 teaspoon garlic powder
- 1 teaspoon onion powder
- Salt and pepper to taste
- Ranch or blue cheese dressing for dipping

Instructions

1. **Preheat Oven:**
   - Preheat oven to 450°F (230°C).
2. **Prepare Batter:**
   - In a bowl, mix flour, garlic powder, onion powder, salt, and pepper. Add enough water to make a batter.
3. **Coat Cauliflower:**
   - Dip cauliflower florets into the batter, then place on a baking sheet lined with parchment paper. Bake for 20 minutes until golden.
4. **Add Sauce:**
   - Toss baked cauliflower in buffalo sauce and return to the oven for an additional 10 minutes. Serve with ranch or blue cheese dressing.

Smoked Mac and Cheese

Ingredients

- 1 lb elbow macaroni
- 4 tablespoons butter
- ¼ cup all-purpose flour
- 4 cups milk
- 4 cups shredded cheese (cheddar, mozzarella, or a blend)
- 1 teaspoon smoked paprika
- Salt and pepper to taste
- Breadcrumbs for topping

Instructions

1. **Cook Macaroni:**
   - Cook macaroni according to package instructions and set aside.
2. **Make Cheese Sauce:**
   - In a saucepan, melt butter over medium heat. Stir in flour and cook for 1 minute. Gradually whisk in milk, cooking until thickened.
3. **Add Cheese:**
   - Remove from heat and stir in cheese, smoked paprika, salt, and pepper until smooth.
4. **Combine and Smoke:**
   - Mix cheese sauce with macaroni, transfer to a smoker-safe dish, and top with breadcrumbs. Smoke for 1 hour at 225°F (107°C) until bubbly.

BBQ Brisket Sandwiches with Slaw

Ingredients

- 1 lb smoked brisket, sliced
- 4 sandwich rolls
- 1 cup coleslaw (store-bought or homemade)
- ½ cup BBQ sauce
- Pickles for garnish

Instructions

1. **Prepare Brisket:**
   - Heat sliced brisket in a skillet over medium heat until warmed through.
2. **Assemble Sandwiches:**
   - On each roll, layer sliced brisket, BBQ sauce, and coleslaw.
3. **Serve:**
   - Serve with pickles on the side.

Grilled Chicken Caesar Salad

Ingredients

- 2 boneless, skinless chicken breasts
- 4 cups romaine lettuce, chopped
- ½ cup Caesar dressing
- ¼ cup grated Parmesan cheese
- Croutons for topping
- Salt and pepper to taste

Instructions

1. **Grill Chicken:**
    - Season chicken breasts with salt and pepper. Grill on medium heat for 6-7 minutes per side until cooked through.
2. **Slice Chicken:**
    - Let chicken rest for a few minutes, then slice.
3. **Assemble Salad:**
    - In a bowl, combine lettuce, Caesar dressing, and Parmesan cheese. Top with grilled chicken and croutons.

Barbecue Glazed Meatball Subs

Ingredients

- 1 lb ground beef or turkey
- 1 cup breadcrumbs
- 1 egg
- 1 teaspoon garlic powder
- 1 cup BBQ sauce
- 4 hoagie rolls
- 1 cup shredded cheese (optional)

Instructions

1. **Make Meatballs:**
    - In a bowl, combine ground meat, breadcrumbs, egg, garlic powder, salt, and pepper. Form into meatballs.
2. **Cook Meatballs:**
    - Bake meatballs at 400°F (200°C) for 20-25 minutes, or until cooked through.
3. **Add Sauce:**
    - Toss cooked meatballs in BBQ sauce.
4. **Assemble Subs:**
    - Place meatballs in hoagie rolls and top with cheese if desired. Serve hot.

BBQ Veggie Pizza

Ingredients

- 1 pizza crust (store-bought or homemade)
- ½ cup BBQ sauce
- 1 cup shredded mozzarella cheese
- 1 cup mixed veggies (bell peppers, red onion, corn, etc.)
- Fresh cilantro for garnish

Instructions

1. **Preheat Oven:**
    - Preheat oven according to pizza crust instructions.
2. **Assemble Pizza:**
    - Spread BBQ sauce over the pizza crust. Top with cheese and mixed veggies.
3. **Bake:**
    - Bake according to crust instructions until cheese is melted and bubbly. Garnish with fresh cilantro before serving.

Grilled Oysters with Garlic Butter

Ingredients

- 12 fresh oysters, shucked
- 4 tablespoons unsalted butter, melted
- 4 cloves garlic, minced
- 1 tablespoon lemon juice
- 2 tablespoons fresh parsley, chopped
- Salt and pepper to taste
- Lemon wedges for serving

Instructions

1. **Preheat Grill:**
    - Preheat the grill to medium-high heat.
2. **Prepare Garlic Butter:**
    - In a bowl, combine melted butter, minced garlic, lemon juice, parsley, salt, and pepper.
3. **Place Oysters on Grill:**
    - Arrange shucked oysters on the grill, flat side up.
4. **Add Garlic Butter:**
    - Spoon garlic butter mixture generously over each oyster.
5. **Grill Oysters:**
    - Close the grill lid and cook for 5-7 minutes, or until the oysters are heated through and the edges begin to curl.
6. **Serve:**
    - Remove from the grill, and serve immediately with lemon wedges.

BBQ Chicken and Cornbread Casserole

Ingredients

- 2 cups cooked chicken, shredded
- 1 cup BBQ sauce
- 1 cup corn kernels (fresh, frozen, or canned)
- 1 cup shredded cheese (cheddar or your choice)
- 1 box cornbread mix (plus ingredients required on the box)
- 1/2 cup milk
- 2 eggs
- 1/2 teaspoon garlic powder
- Salt and pepper to taste

Instructions

1. **Preheat Oven:**
    - Preheat the oven to 375°F (190°C).
2. **Mix Chicken Mixture:**
    - In a large bowl, combine shredded chicken, BBQ sauce, corn, half of the cheese, garlic powder, salt, and pepper. Spread the mixture evenly in a greased 9x13-inch baking dish.
3. **Prepare Cornbread:**
    - In another bowl, prepare the cornbread mix according to package instructions, adding milk and eggs. Stir until just combined.
4. **Pour Cornbread Batter:**
    - Pour the cornbread batter over the chicken mixture in the baking dish.
5. **Bake:**
    - Bake for 25-30 minutes, or until the cornbread is golden and cooked through.
6. **Add Cheese:**
    - Remove from the oven, sprinkle the remaining cheese on top, and return to the oven for an additional 5-10 minutes until the cheese is melted and bubbly.
7. **Serve:**
    - Let cool slightly before serving. Enjoy warm!

www.ingramcontent.com/pod-product-compliance
Lightning Source LLC
LaVergne TN
LVHW081331060526
838201LV00055B/2568